EXPELLING *the* BEAST
FROM WITHIN

By
Crystalline Ray

Columbia, South Carolina

Copyright@2016 by Crystalline Ray

Expelling the Beast from Within by Crystalline Ray

All rights reserved. This book is protected by the copyright laws of the United States of America. This book may not be copied or reprinted for personal gain or profit. The use of short quotations or occasional page copying for personal or group study is permitted and encouraged. Permission will be granted upon request. Unless otherwise identified, Scripture quotations are from the King James Version. Copyright © 1982 Thomas Nelson Inc. Used by permission. All rights reserved. Please note that this author and Change Publishers publishing style capitalizes certain pronouns that refer to the Father, Son, and Holy Spirit.

Cover photo by TaraPatta courtesy Shutterstock.com. Additional vector designs courtesy Pixabay.com.

ISBN #978-1-7322629-3-5
Change Publishers Columbia, SC 29229
Changepublishers@gmail.com
Printed in the United States of America First Printing, 2020

Dedication

I dedicate this book to my Lord and Savior Jesus Christ. I also dedicate it to all the people whose lives that will be changed for the better by reading this book.

Foreword

Crystalline Ray—what a super obedient and faithful woman of God with an enlightening flair for writing. In *Expelling the Beast from Within* she gives an insightful glance into the spirit realm where an invisible and relentless war is being levied against mankind. Crystalline brings this realm into focus so that we can see and understand scripturally the enemy we face; his mind, thoughts, schemes, and strongholds. How he manipulates our thoughts through suggestion and fear.

Crystalline thoroughly examines the way we travel through life totally oblivious to this spiritual battle that goes on for our mind, will, and emotions. She reveals how the end goal of the enemy is to bring us to our knees, render us helpless, ineffective, and unable to carry out Gods plans and purposes for our lives.

Though fighting an invisible enemy seems to be impossible, Crystalline reveals how to face and defeat this enemy by way of our champion and defender, Jesus Christ.

Ty Green

Acknowledgements

I would like to acknowledge my remarkable husband for his support in everything I do. I appreciate his labor of love for the Kingdom of God and his devotion to our family.

I acknowledge my wonderful children, their spouses, their children, and generations to come. Thanks to my good friends Lee and Ty for their dedication and hard work.

Thanks to the Change Publishers team because they are an impressive group of men and women to work with. I thank each one of them for all their hard work and labor of excellence.

Introduction

We are in a war!

We find ourselves fighting a war we never knew existed. There is an unseen world with unseen powers. These powers are stealth and wage opposition against us without our knowledge. The effects of this conflict are felt both individually and worldwide. So, we are in a battle and because we do not know our enemy, it seems as if we are already defeated. It is called spiritual warfare.

This spiritual battle is waged in the earth realm by spiritual foes which are principalities, powers, and rulers of the darkness of this world, with spiritual wickedness in high places (Ephesians 6:12).

Their mission is to seek, find our weakness, kill, steal, and destroy (John 10:10). Their plan is to control us through mind control, to overthrow, and possess our wills. As seducers of the mind, they tempt, deceive, intimidate, and dominate us. Their seduction causes fear, which opens doors to depression and oppression.

Mr. Nash, the main character in this book, asks "How will I overcome these master spirits which I cannot see?"

Contents

Chapter 1—The Fight 13

Chapter 2—Vexed 19

Chapter 3—Believe 23

Chapter 4—Power From On High 29

Chapter 5—Face Your Fears 37

Chapter 6—Advance With Confidence 41

Chapter 7—Sweet, Sweet Victory! 45

Chapter 8—The Truth That Sets You Free 53

Decision 57

Round One

The Fight

Down, but not out.

I did not initiate this fight! This feels like a nightmare. When my contender silently entered the arena without grandeur, his stature did not go unnoticed. He appears to stand about ten feet tall and weigh 600 pounds. Although there are no bells and whistles, there is a slight tremble below my feet. I am confused while watching him. He appears to move around without his feet touching the ground. He pauses in front of me, and my heartbeat explodes inside my chest.

Although I know that I am not alone, I feel dreadfully alone. In slow motion he removes the hood that covers his grotesque face which causes my feeling of loneliness to intensify. An ominous shadow appears, enveloping the surrounding light. He looks like an experiment gone wrong, part human and part beast; altered by genetic engineering. Deformed, deep ripples of muscles rip from his body. The deep brown hair that drapes around his face resembles the mane of a lion. The negative energy that fills our surroundings appears to invigorate him with intense pleasure.

A smirk engulfs his face as he takes deep, long breaths while moving his head from side to side. He circles his hands in front of his nostrils, appearing to be intoxicated with the stench he inhales. What is this power it has over me? There have been many giants in my life, but this one thing I have yet to overcome.

The mere presence of this thing makes me feel like a failure and defeated. He lunges forward, speaking negative, filthy, and abrasive words. As I nervously jerk backward, I lose my balance and stumble. He punches with an uppercut to the face; I fall. He circles me like a wild beast taunting his prey before the kill. His evil presence hovers over me. The foul stench of his breath makes my nostrils burn. I wipe away the sweat that causes my eyes to sting. Seeing him through the pain of my half-open eyes, he looks like a massive black shadow. His glowing red eyes pierce the darkness with raging fury.

With every tick of the clock, my heart pounds with fear. I take long, slow, deep breaths as my weak, limp body is in a slump. He moves away; I rest one arm across the ropes.

The Fight

I'm hot, sticky, and drenched in sweat. I try to support my exhausted body over the ropes as my bruised right shoulder burns intensely. Slowly, I lift my left knee to regain balance. In my weakened state, I realize I have been in this position before. It makes me feel like a trapped animal instinctively struggling to be free.

In the past, I have made it out slightly bruised but alive. However, this time I am not sure. Gasping for breath, I take a moment to regain my composure. Every time I try to gain control, he lashes out. He is pure evil, *massive, strong, and ugly*. His negative words bring me to a low place, shredding my self-esteem. His tactics are working. He is like a ferocious animal out of control. When they smell fear, it heightens their desire to kill.

He swings and hits me in the face; I am down. My right hand trembles uncontrollably as I hold on to the ropes, trying to lift my body. The pain is unbearable. He pounds me with brute force, and I can taste salt and blood as the sweat pours down my face. The impact of his punches feels like a semi-truck advancing at full speed. Nausea and dizziness cloud my thoughts. Life mistakes flash before my eyes.

I hear distant voices of people encouraging me not to give up but fight back. Eerie noises send waves of distress up and down my spine. Every hair on my body stands on end.

Expelling the Beast

Negative energy covers me like a blanket, keeping me bound in fear. It feels more like a presence than a physical state of being. I feel trapped with no hope of escape.

This darkness overwhelms me and makes me think of death. He sucker-punches me, knocking the breath out of me. The punch brings me to my knees. The faint voices are saying, *"Get up! Get up! You can do it! It's not over yet!"* They do not understand. I hear them and want to get up, but I cannot. This is not a favorable disposition, but I cannot seem to leave it. With every movement, my body hurts.

I feel broken.

It breaks my will.

I am broken!

I never knew I could feel so lost and hopeless.

This needs to end now!

But he would win. Something on the inside will not let me give up. With every breath I take, I feel something deep inside, fueling me with fresh energy. With the referee's every count, I acknowledge the urge to stand. The only reason he has not counted me out is I am still holding on to the rope; therefore, legally I am still standing. The way I feel at this moment, the referee can call it off. He will not because he sees I have not fully surrendered. His voice is gentle as he slowly counts. This appears to calm the beast. It is amazing, even during this fight

The Fight

for my life, the referee's presence brings peace. With every continued count, something on the inside of me yells, *"Get up Benjamin, get up!"*

How is this done in a weakness? With every blow, my opponent has drained me. Struggling to stand causes me to slip down.

I Feel woozy; but maybe if I do not focus on the pain, I can get up. Hearing the voices of encouragement makes me realize that I need help! I hear the referee, but I am struggling! I hear my opponent breathing perversely. My body trembles. There is a distinct voice on the inside which speaks louder than the others I have heard before. I have never totally yielded to it, but today it is clearer than ever. With every word, I feel a surge of strength. Those words bring hope and the desire to fight. They produce an assurance which makes me feel like I can win this battle.

I can and will get up.

I will focus on the voice from the inside—not my pain, not my brokenness, but that voice. This opponent is relentless; with every move I make, he tries to attack me. The referee prevents him from advancing by reminding him of the rules. On my feet again, but still unstable.

The bell rings. *Thank God!*

Round Two

Vexed

Keep your focus on the win.

I stagger back to my side of the ring.

Barely seeing through my watery eyes, I feel the comfort of my trainer's arms as he grabs my right arm and puts it around his neck. He tells me to rest my weight on him, so I shift my weight, and he moves me swiftly and safely to the other side. He quickly washes away the blood and the sweat and applies a soothing balm to manage the pain. The cold metal of the eye iron pressed against my face is a welcome relief and helps to keep the swelling down.

I feel the warmth of my trainer's rough hands when he cups my face to get my total attention because I still look and feel dazed. Diverting my attention, the beast hisses, and I lock eyes on him as I sit there. He stares at me with wrinkled brows, lips curled, and teeth gritted. His deep-set coppery red eyes seem to speak to me saying, *"This is your last round. I will take you out!"*

He jumps up into the ropes, braces himself, and throws his arms in the air and shakes his fist. He continually flexes his muscles, spewing a barrage of profanity.

The trainer helps me to recharge and reminds me of why I was born. He speaks positive words of affirmation into my life, reminding me of my dreams and goals. He encourages me to see past my present condition, causing me to adjust my way of thinking. Instead of failure and defeat, I must condition myself to have a winner's attitude; with the understanding that my destiny is in my hands. He reminds me to have faith in my God-given abilities and to be strong and courageous. He recites stories of mighty warriors, who kept pressing through many of the same challenges I have faced and were victorious.

He has my undivided attention as I quietly listen. The inside voice softly agrees with my trainer's words, so I begin to believe him. As my belief increases, I can feel my strength increasing. I feel revived and refreshed, and I am ready to take the challenge once more.

However, my question is, where is God and where was he when my wife died? She died in a tragic car accident three years ago. I still find it hard to deal with. The pain still overwhelms me. She meant the world to me. I feel drained and

Vexed

lost. I cannot help but feel like it is my fault. If only I did not value making money over a forty-five-minute drive, she would still be here with me today. Not picking her up for the social event was the mistake I made. I chose to work overtime and meet her there. That day plays over and over in my head. My best friend is lost forever, and I am finding it hard to live without her.

It broke my heart beyond repair. Living will never be the same because I chose to make money over her.

Those dreadful words repeat in my mind. "Sorry, Mr. Nash, your wife did not make it."

The bell rings. The break is over.

That beast comes out of the corner and swings wildly.

How in the world do I stop this wild beast?

Standing before the most fearful thing on earth; but he is just a beast. Failing in this position before, I keep trying.

Why did I allow my trainer to persuade me to fight again?

Why am I so afraid, and why do I allow this beast to torment me? Knowing the odds are against me, I am determined to defy them. This fear cannot be allowed to hold me hostage forever.

Well, I cannot back down now. Okay, I must focus! I guess I can answer my question. The choice is life and not death. I quickly maneuver out of his way this time because he swings uncontrollably. He steps forward with a rock and slight dance; he misses, then jumps back and forth.

He moves his head from side to side, pushes out his chest and rushes in with force, aiming for the kill. Moving quickly to the left, to avoid his punch, he doubles back with a left uppercut! Noticing the blood smeared on his glove, it shows evidence that my lip is split. As my trembling legs give way, I begin to doubt myself, and that is when I fall. Something keeps pushing me to keep going. I get up.

Moving around the ropes, I rotate my arms and shoulders, trying to release the tension and pain. Am I crazy? Yes, I can imagine that the beast thinks so. He laughs at me and my attempts. His continuous laughing throws him off balance and I realize this is a striking moment! His domination can end right now! Mounting up every morsel of strength left in my painful body, I throw a cross punch. *"Yes!"* Slowly my glove hits his hideous face and sweat showers the air as he adjusts to the left. He looks dazed but brushes it off.

The bell is sweet music to my ears. My imaginary crowd goes wild! Sighing with relief, I wipe sweat from my brow. Making it through another round, I feel good and stride back to my corner with assurance. I wave my raised arms in the air and shake them for approval. Positive energy is vibrating through my veins.

Round Three

Believe

I must believe in myself.

When I returned to my corner, I intentionally ignored the beast and paid close attention to my trainer. It elated me when he told me I did well, but believing in myself is not enough. To win this fight, I must confess and believe in a greater power than me.

Therefore, I must believe I can prevail. All the words spoken by him mean nothing if I do not act upon them. He said if I want to change my life, I must change my actions.

"It's time to stop putting it off. I must believe in the power that is greater than even the beast." "What? There is a power greater than this beast?" I questioned. "Well, now that I think about it, I have always heard there is a greater power, but I am not sure any power is greater than what I am going through.

To overcome this torment, I will push my doubts aside and just believe."

"Do it because you value your life and where you will spend eternity," said the trainer.

Perplexed, I looked at him and said, "I do not plan to die today." *What does eternity have to do with darkness?*

He looked at me and said, "I know no one plans to die, but it can and may happen when you are not expecting it."

Okay, I ponder his statement and conclude he may be right. His words seem correct so far. I confess, I believe there is a power greater than the beast. After my confession, he informs me that I need to surrender my life to this power.

"What do you mean, 'surrender'?" I asked.

"When you surrender to Him, your life becomes empowered with His dunamis power; your life becomes His life. He lives through you. No matter what *beast* you face in this life, the power within will help you overcome it."

As I stood, my trainer continues to say, "Begin now to trust the greater power within." *How do I trust if I do not know how?*

The Bell rings. Here we go again.

Stepping into the ring, perplexed, and still thinking about what my trainer said, I accepted the Greater One in my life and believe He is a force greater than this beast.

Without a doubt, I must know that I can win, and I am a

Believe

winner. Wow, that is deep!

Repeating these words as I try to bob and weave and move along the ropes quickly. Covering my face as I duck and dodge blows, I just want to feel like a winner.

Normally the beast comes back from the corner with his fists raised for the punch, but he stops, looks at me with a crazed look, steps backs and roars loudly. The sound ripples from the top of his head to the soles of his feet, causing his entire body to vibrate. He paces back and forth like he is considering his next move.

This is confusing because he has never done that before. He has always rushed in with blows or with mockery. He uses intimidation and fear. He continues to roar as he surrounds me like a wild animal. The sound is more frightening than his appearance.

What did I do?

Is it time for me to run for my life! I cannot because something within me will not allow it. Frozen with fear, my feet feel glued to the floor. He runs toward me with his fists up, ready to pound me. Shifting my body to the right, he misses. His roar is so loud, it is deafening, so I cover my ears. He seizes another opportunity to throw another punch; It makes contact but does not faze me.

He is furious. Something is different this time around. My

trainer yells, "Believe in the power within!" The beast hears him and stops in his tracks. He walks over to my trainer and roars. Fearless confidence rises in me, and I move swiftly to the same corner.

With a disgusted look, the beast turns around and swings quickly at me. Ducking in time, he misses. He quickly swings again knocking me off balance; he smiles.

After gaining my footing, the beast knocks me down again. He then stands over me with his fist balled tightly and I see a blur as he prepares to strike.

The bell stops him in full swing. I feel the brush of air close to my face as he pounds the swinging fist into his glove and turns and walks to his corner. He stomps and curses on the way back.

I struggle to breathe as my chest heaves up and down. Hearing those voices again, yelling *don't give up, and hang in there*, makes me frustrated and discouraged as I walk to my corner of the ring.

"Have faith!" my trainer yells.

"What is faith?" I asked in an agitated voice.

He says, "It's not a feeling, and it may not be rational. You cannot touch it; you must believe in it, although you cannot see it. It is laying hold of what you believe but cannot see, touch, or feel. You must see it in the spiritual realm before you will bring it into the natural realm. Then it becomes reality."

"What? I can believe I am getting my behind kicked all over the ring. Now that's a reality!"

"Now, now, let me explain," exclaimed my trainer.

"Please do," I frown at him.

"Faith is action, acting on your belief. It is being confident in what you hope for; to overcome and be convinced in what you do not see: the victory! You must believe in the greater power within you to win. No matter how bad it is, you must always see yourself as a winner and not a loser."

See yourself the way God sees you then no beast in hell can stop you from becoming the winner God has called you to be. Always remember the stories of the mighty warriors I have told you repeatedly. It was through faith they conquered kings and kingdoms. They shut the mouth of the lion and escaped the edge of the sword."

Listening quietly, I absorb his words while still wondering where God was before my wife died.

"Now, all I want to know about is the victory part. How can I win? That is all I want to know." "Believe" he whispered.

Round Four

Power From On High

What is the greater power within?

How can I have faith like those mighty warriors? Does it have something to do with the voice I hear? Oh! Here comes the beast! This time I will try something different. Speaking aloud the words my trainer told me. The beast stares at me with a look of amusement. I stare back without saying a word. Never have I spoken to him before. I have always allowed him to dominate me within the ring with his negative words. He repeats the words I say. He continues to taunt me, step by step. "I will win, and you will fail," I exclaim. "You are the ugliest and the vilest thing I have ever seen." He raises one eyebrow and says, "You are an ugly beast!" "I will knock the smirk off of your hideous face," I say under my breath. He hears me and grins. "I am a winner; not a loser," I repeat. His expression changes. He stops walking and stares at me. His deep red eyes appear to glow like golden explosive flames. He says, "You are not who you think you are. You were born a loser, and you will always be a loser. I will defeat you this time and every time! I control your feelings and thoughts! I have complete control over you!"

Until this point, he controlled me, so now my struggle is to believe he no longer has control over me. The fight is on.

I swing.

He swings.

I miss.

He hits.

He swings.

I swing.

He misses.

I hit.

This made me tired, and I think it frustrated the beast. Tilting his head back while shaking it from side to side, a loud piercing roar escapes his lips. He prances around spewing discouraging words. They are abusive, callous, and distressing; intending to press me down and impede my movement. This time I will not allow words to press me down. I am vulnerable to his attacks and do not have the strength to fight him alone. Because I need help I have no choice but to believe in the greater power within. At that moment, something stirs inside of me. "Greater is He who is in me than he who is in the world," I say aloud.

The battle has picked up. We throw blow after blow. Sweat is everywhere. As the fight intensifies, the beast is all over me. He does not let up. I feel the burden of his presence; but I can also feel fresh energy as I move. It is an inexplicable feeling that comes from the depths of my soul. Greater is He that rises within me. I believe it!

As I confess these words aloud, we continue to exchange blows. I feel every blow, but I am determined to press through the pain. The words the beast projects cause mental and emotional anguish. It feels like a sword piercing and turning inside me at the same time. In my failed state, I want to stop and give up, but something keeps driving me.

Greater is He!

Greater is He!

Greater is He!

Confessing, this makes me feel like I am in a zone, boxing like a champion. Adrenaline rushes over me as I imagine a crowd of people here applauding, waving flags, jumping up and down, and cheering me on.

Unfortunately, I lose focus on the fight because my thoughts are on the cheers. They empower me. I feel invincible and it overshadows my focus on the greater one and causes my ego to swell. *It's all about you and me, you don't need the greater one".*

The beast says in a seductive voice. It is all about me; I agree with the beast. I do not need the greater one; I can do this all myself. All I needed was the imaginary crowd to begin to cheer me on. Therefore, I am still standing.

After saying these words aloud, something shifts, and a smile comes over the beast's face. He knows something I do not. The fight takes a turn for the worst. The beast beats the life out of me. Blood is on his gloves; he pulverizes me and throws me around like a rag doll. He is irate, and the referee intervenes, standing between us, holding him back. The beast is trying to jump over his back, uttering profanity toward me.

He shouted "you are nothing and will never amount to anything. You have the audacity to come out and take a stand against me. Who do you think you are? I control you! I told you! I told you!"

His abrasive words pierced my soul and drained my strength.

The bell rings.

Needing help to get to my corner, my trainer appears in a matter of seconds. Shaking his head at me, he escorts me back to the corner.

"What were you thinking? You did so well out there. What happened?" Spitting blood out of my mouth, I mumbled, "I don't know." I don't know what happened. The cheers from the crowd made me feel like I was on cloud nine."

Coughing up more blood, I said, "They were the reason I was still standing."

"Hush now. Let me fix you up," said my trainer as he explains that my words have power. He told me that I am a spirit being living in a natural world. Words are spiritual; therefore, they bring life to this natural world. They take form in the atmosphere and manifest here in the natural realm. Whether negative or positive, they affect my attitude, feelings, and whether I fail or succeed. Evil spirits coupled with the negative words I speak control the beast. He thrives off the negative and manifests through my fears, doubts, and unbeliefs. He is an ancient foe and is knowledgeable in his craft.

He hears my negative words, and he uses them to destroy me. He continues to explain how the beast grew in stature and strength when I said I did not need the greater one to help me. Those words gave the beast authority and power over me, but I still have the greater power within.

"You must allow the greater power to control your thoughts, which will help you control the words you speak. He is the one who will give you the arsenal to subdue the beast, not the crowd! Make no mistake; he can work through a crowd to boost your ego. Words of encouragement always make you feel good but understand where your true strength comes from."

"It's not the crowd."

"I don't understand. Why does it matter? If the crowd's cheering makes me feel empowered, then why is it a problem?"

"Sometimes your feelings can fool you," said my trainer.

"What?" I questioned.

"Yes," he replied, "Sometimes your feelings fool you. For example, you wake up in the morning feeling sad and low in spirit. As a result, negative thoughts enter your mind. You allow those negative thoughts to penetrate your heart, and then you come under the influence of the spirit of depression. Once it enters your heart, your feelings can deceive you into believing you will never win, and the world is against you. You then speak aloud that this life is not worth living and you will never amount to anything. You feel you are here to live, then die accomplishing nothing. You believe this so strongly; its proclamation shapes your atmosphere and stalls your future victories. Under the influence of depression, you do not feel motivated to try anything old or new. Therefore, you must not allow your negative feelings to consume you. You must know in your heart that they are only there to support you and not to empower you. You must also learn to train your mind to think on things that are true, just, pure, and of good report."

Absorbing what he says, I look straight ahead and say, "I

feel there is something different about this fight." "If you can believe and rely on the greater power within, you have a chance at winning this time. Do you understand me?"

With a nod, I acknowledged him.

He picks up a book and reads. He then asks me to repeat his words. "You are a conqueror, and you are victorious. Always remember the greater power of which I speak has helped hundreds of warriors, even when it looked like they should have failed. When they lack physical strength, The Greater One strengthened them through His power. You too are a mighty warrior. Believe it or not, you are a mighty warrior according to the words of the greater one. There is no feat too great for you to overcome with Him on your side." As I listen to his words, tears of joy well up inside me. There is something so powerful, amazing, and true about his words. I feel calm and the words begin to energize me. It is as if they are alive. Not only do they bring peace, but they also bring hope. They calm my spirit, subside my fears, and help me see past what I face in this ring.

I want to sit and listen, however, it's not a choice right now; I must continue to fight for my freedom. One thing I have learned in life is freedom is not free; you must fight for it.

At that moment, my trainer says, "You must confront all your fears." I feel as if he could read my mind.

Round Five

Face Your Fears

Casting down negative imaginations.

Why would this power, I don't understand, help me fight a beast larger than I am? I questioned. My trainer says "our measure cannot define Him, but I will attempt to describe Him". He is the invisible *God, holy and true.* The Creator of the world; The source of all life and being. He holds many titles. He is eternal, steadfast, imperial, gracious, unmovable, all-knowing, and all-wise. He is all-powerful, and there is nothing too hard for Him. He is The King of Heaven; The Everlasting God; Creator and Redeemer; King of Righteousness; Supreme ruler; Shepherd and Our Righteousness; The King of Glory. He is matchless; no one in this world compares to Him.

He is a Servant to all. He is the only one who qualifies as the all-sufficient Savior. His love is limitless, and He never changes. His mercy is everlasting, and His grace is enough. He is a rewarder to them that diligently seek Him. He holds wisdom and the key to all knowledge. He is everywhere.

Now, I hope you understand that He is the one who has made you; He created you after His own image and likeness. You are valuable to Him. He bought your freedom with His blood. When He formed you in your mother's womb, He equipped you to be a conqueror. When He made you, He gave you authority over everything that concerns you. You cannot live the abundant life without Him.

This fight that you are in is not a physical fight, but a spiritual fight. You need Him to defeat the beast you see before you today. He equipped you with spiritual weapons when you were born. Activation started when you gave your life to Him. You were equipped with the Power of the All Mighty God. The beast can magnify negative imagery which plants itself into your mind, plays over and over, and eventually weakens you.

All your greatest fears become a part of your imaginations. The beast is a master mind bender. He takes these images, twist them into his plan for your life. He will prophesy suggestions of dreadful things that can happen. I repeat! They are images formed in your mind of horrible things that can happen to you. The beast fights you in your mind. He sets up strongholds that oppose you and the plans of God for your life. These things may never happen, however, the beast uses them to paralyze you and it will stop you from advancing. He also uses them as obstacles

Face Your Fears

to slow your progress in anything you attempt to do. So, again, you must face your fears! This time, when you face the beast, remember, he stands between you and greatness; between you and your freedom! He stands between you and your dreams! He constantly reminds you of past failures and pain, but you must know and genuinely believe you are a winner and not a loser. Speak it aloud! *"Greater is He who is in me, than my doubts and fears!"* You must face them with a winner's attitude; don't give up and never quit!"

"But coach!" "The beast is real to me. He is not a figment of my imagination, and I have the wounds to prove it. If you look closely, this is actual blood, and I hurt! How can I believe past the hurt and pain?"

He replied, "If you are not willing to let go of your hurt, you will continue to suffer from the pain. Let me say it like this. If you are not willing to let go of the things causing bondage, your torment will continue. The only things that restrain you are your fears, and you choosing to entertain the negative. When the negative images first enter your thoughts, you have a choice to make, either you will entertain them, meditate on them, or counter them."

You received them and did not block them out of your mind or counter the negative with positive thoughts. You accepted the negative as factual; therefore, negative thinking can and will overwhelm your mind, it presses down on you. That is why you feel depressed. Your fears have overshadowed your self-image. Now you see yourself as the beast wants you to see. You agree with the negative thoughts and lose sight of your dreams. You feel comfortable in that present position, yet you are miserable, but what have you done to relieve it?"

"That is not true," I yell, "I am not comfortable, hurting yes, but not comfortable." "Well, have you asked for help?"

"No, I responded, but I…"

He cuts in and says, "That says it all. You have never inquired."

"No, I guess I never inquired. Where would I go and who would understand?" The trainer continues, "There are many people in this world who will understand your fears. Thousands of them have the same problem. Some have come into this knowledge and mastered their speech, and some are still working on it. Counselors can help, but the greatest help of all comes from the "Chief Physician." He knows your present condition. If you can only *believe* in what I have told you about Him and how He will help you, you can *win*. You must cast down the negative imaginations. You can take and replace the negative thought pattern with the words of the Greater One. Open your mouth and decree and declare what this book says about you. Understand today the Lord your God is He who goes before you as a consuming fire. He will destroy the beast and bring him down before you" What an amazing God! I am amazed.

Round Six

Confidence

I must advance with confidence.

He is more than I could ever imagine. It is a little hard to believe everything my trainer said about Him, and all this greatness lives inside of me. I only have a few seconds to put everything into perspective. I sense the presence of hate as I enter the ring this time. The beast is mad; I know it is because I am still standing. Determined not to let him win, I will not!

As I enter the ring, I swing. The beast stands and looks at me like I am a madman. He swats at me, like a cat playing with a ball of yarn, as if he is amused by my tactics. There is a mixture of fear and determination as I advance with knowledge and confidence. Determined to face my fears and win, my body feels tense and my nerves flutter. Finally, I realize there is a fight going on inside and outside. I am battling for my life, and must fight through all adversities. Because I allowed my surroundings to affect the way I feel, negative influences have taken residence in my heart and mind. These feelings dictated what my mood would be like for that day.

I must believe the knowledge that was revealed to me is true. Therefore, I will no longer allow my imagination to magnify the way the beast wants me to see him. Now that I know the truth about him, I am determined to see him for who he is. He is not ten feet tall, not even six hundred pounds. Believing he is not greater than the power that lives inside me is a keen insight and a fresh revelation.

This belief in the greater power outweighs how I see the beast. Now, I will fight him with a clear vision. I understand that I cannot continue to have faith in what I see with my natural eyes as factual. If only I can believe beyond my natural mind and allow my spirit to connect with the greater power to prevail in my life. The Greater One gives insight into every situation. Tapping into the spirit realm by faith, I must yield myself to Him and ask for guidance.

I know the truth about myself, I will no longer allow a depressed state to dominate my life. Mastering this task will take time, but I am determined to make it happen. I am in the fight for my life. Let me take a moment and pray. *Father, I bow down and humble myself before You today. Teach me to pray. My*

Confidence

life is in Your hands. Have mercy on me and teach me Your ways. Lead me in Your plain path. I want to know you in the depts of my heart. I put my trust in You. Consider my trouble. Please forgive me, for I have spent a part of my life consumed with grief. I was mad at You and this world. I blamed you for the death of my wife.

Pull me out of the hands of this enemy for he has oppressed me daily. Bow down Your ear and deliver me speedily. Be my rock and a house of defense. You are my shield and buckler. Pull me up and out of despair. Deliver me from the will of my enemy and the trap he has set for me. Draw out your sword and stop him that oppresses me.

Make this enemy that has come up against me to stumble and fall. Scatter him by Your power and bring him down. Confound him and put him to shame. Let him be turned back and brought to confusion because he devises to hurt me. He hid a net in a pit for my destruction. Ambush him and let him be caught in the very net he has set for me. Let him be as shaft before the wind.

Free me now from all hidden traps. Give me a keen spirit so I will not fall into the trap of the enemy again. Hide me in Your secret place. You are my refuge, fortress, strong tower, and very present help in time of trouble. In You I am safe. I will not be afraid of the disease that prowls through the darkness, nor the disaster that erupts at high noon. I decree and declare because I *have made You my God and Lord, no evil will befall me, neither shall any plague come nigh my dwelling. For You have given Your angels charge over me.*

My soul shall be joyful in You my God. I rejoice in my salvation. I celebrate Your great works in my life. I sing because there is no one like You. No one can compare or even come close to You and Your works. You are the lifter of my head. I am strengthened in You. You called me out of darkness into the marvelous light. You delivered me for an enemy that was too strong for me. You cause my soul to be free and elevated from oppression and depression.

I give You thanks. I will declare Your glory all day long. I will open my mouth wide and proclaim Your goodness. In You I put my trust.

Round Seven

Sweet, Sweet Victory

There is a sweetness in victory.

Suddenly the beast takes a quick look at me, then focuses his attention on the referee and shouts, with an eerie cry of rage, *"That's not fair; he belongs to me! I claim what is mine!"* The referee yelled back, "Jesus claimed him from the foundation of the world; He paid the ultimate price when He died for mankind's sins on the cross!" Red smoke rises from his nostrils as ghastly sinister screams rise from his throat. With furious bursts of rage, the massive beast runs behind the referee. He wails profane and outlandish accusations about me. The referee yells at the beast. "You know the rules! Those things were in his past. They no longer exist; the blood of Jesus covers them. Jesus was wounded for his transgression, bruised for his iniquities, and again you know the rules!" "Bump the rules! I demand the right to have him! So, back off and allow me access to his soul!" The referee shakes his head and says, "No, no, I cannot change what God set in motion from the beginning of time." The beast stomps his right foot and continues rambling. *"He is mine and I will finish him today!* He is feeble. His will to live was broken when he lost his wife three years ago. He sought comfort in the bottle instead of your God. I deceived him into believing money was his god, and I toyed with his emotions until now. This is the day I schemed and planned to devour him. Mesmerized with the evil pleasures of this world, he grew up believing that he could buy people at any price."

While rubbing his hands together with a smirk on his face, he says, "He fell into every trap I set for him. He was s-o-o-o easy. I was successful in keeping his mind filled with this world system instead of your God. His soul is void of religion. So, stop trying to fill it now. Wooing him was easy; I kept his eyes, and mind focused on himself. I used all kinds of devices and tricks—television, movies, and my specialty, *music*. Your God sent one preacher after another. He even sent angels to aid. He shrugged them off then as I plan to shrug you off today. He did not waste time with your God's words. I jammed his mind every chance I got, so I could program my agenda, not your God. "I am good at what I do." "Jesus paid the ransom on the cross. He has accepted, believed, and acknowledged Jesus as Lord over his life!" The referee yelled back.

Sweet, Sweet Victory

The beast turned his head quickly to refocus his attention on me and through his clenched teeth he muffled his words mixed with growls. "Give up. You are nothing. You cannot win. You will not win. Shattering you will be my pleasure!" He continues to spew out allegations against me. He reminds me of everything I have done wrong in the past. He then turns his attention back to the referee and says, "I won't play by the rules this time. Why does your God even care about these weak, mindless, helpless creatures? Today I will have my way and I claim his soul on this day." Go tell your God to stay out of this one. I built a strong garrison in his mind and fertilized it with despair, making him everything God hates."

The beast prances inside the ring and counts on his finger as he says, "He is selfish, lustful, and greedy. He is no use to you. I have targeted and manipulated him for a long time; I have him right where I want him, and I demand what is rightfully mine!"

"I reiterate today when he asked for forgiveness and made Jesus Lord over his life everything changed for him. Jesus washed away all his sins, and he is a new creature."

At that moment, he made a sudden move toward me out of desperation. He mumbled on his way towards me, "Get out of my way, I will not play by the rules." I meet his advance toward me and swing. He tried to duck, but he was not quick enough. The moment my glove touches his face, there was an intense, illuminating light. It hit the top of his head like a lightning bolt and he falls. For the first time in my life, he falls! There was a slight rumble under my feet. It made me stop in amazement at how hard he hit the ground. Looking up toward heaven, I saw a blaze of light where there was once darkness.

I stop to recognize that this God is exceptional and nothing and no one is, was or will ever be greater. Looking down at my gloves, I shake my head in approval. I feel like I am in another zone and I could hear beads of sweat pour off my face and land on the mat. He gives me the confidence, courage, and strength I need over this situation. He also gives wisdom and knowledge on how to fight and defeat this enemy.

Now that I am boxing and saying the name of my God, Jesus, out of pure gratitude; I notice at the mention of the name Jesus; the beast trembled.

"Who is this God who causes this enemy to tremble at the mention of His name? Who is this God who supersedes everything that has me bound?"

I continued to speak His name as we fight; realizing without Him this would not have been possible. He is the Lord, strong and mighty in battle. He is incomparable; there is no god like the Lord God Almighty!

I feel light on my feet as I dance around the ring, beating

the hell out of this beast. The more I hit him, the less power he has over me. He falls and has not landed a successful blow yet. He stumbles and sways as he tries to get up. Sweat pours from his brows as he growls profane words at me. For once in my life, his words do not have any impact. They do not affect me the way they once did. They have no power over me. Now, I hear them, but I refuse to receive them. I speak what the Word of God says about me. His tactics have failed. The more words I speak, the fainter his voice becomes. He tries to run away from me.

Jesus has enlarged His presence in my life as I believe and speak His words. The beast is agitated and cannot endure it. Where there was darkness, now there is light. *Jesus* is the light of my life, and darkness cannot stay. The light blinds the beast. Not bothered by him, I continue to speak these words with authority:

"Decreeing and declaring that I am a winner and I triumph over my enemies. Victory and the glory of the Lord fills my life. The joy of my God strengthens me.

Because of the blood of the Lamb and the words I speak, I will overcome. I can and will do all things through Christ who strengthens me. I praise God because it is He who causes my hands to war and my fingers to fight. He makes me run through troops and leap over walls.

Expelling the Beast

The spirit of power, love and a sound mind belong to me.
A soundness of mind is my portion.
Victory in Christ Jesus I claim".

Every word confounds the beast; he is in a state of confusion. He shakes his head in disapproval and covers his ears, saying, "No! No! No! Shut up!"

This battle is amazing! Somehow, I see my gloves in the form of a sword every time I hit the beast. It looks like light piercing through darkness. His voice now sounds like he has inhaled helium. He appears smaller and smaller. He is no longer larger than life to me. The tables have turned, and his words no longer consume my thoughts. He shivers in fear and defeat. The voice of Jesus is magnified over the voice of the beast. The Lord is my deliverer, my strength, in whom I will trust.

No longer afraid of the beast, and I intend to make him concede. As I approach him for the last time. I wonder if he sees the determination in my face as he lifts the ropes and tries to run under them. As he puts one leg through the ropes, a flash of lightning hits him, piercing his entire body with light. He arches his back and bends backward, screaming and exploding from within, causing the entire room to illuminate.

The sudden burst of blinding light causes my arm to cover my bloodshot eyes and I can hear faint sounds proclaiming the word of God. Victory, victory, sweet, sweet, victory!

"Arise, shine; for thy light is come, and the glory of the Lord is risen upon thee." (Isaiah 60:1) A warm sensation comes over me. The bottom of the floor gives way under my feet. Those words continue to come forth with power and force, *"Get up from your place of desolation and misery!"* As I struggle to catch my breath, my heart is beating fast, and I realize my clothes are drenched with sweat. These words are so clear, *"Stop wallowing in the darkness — of fear, guilt, and sin!"*

Opening my eyes, I focus my attention on the sun shining through my bay window. A voice from my radio says, *"Wake up from a distressed, depressed state, for the glory of the Lord thy God has entered. Press toward the mark of the high call of Christ Jesus, for He is your savior and your Redeemer. He bought you for a price, and you are no longer your own. So, live your life to please God."*

Wow! Was this all a dream? It felt so real and still resounds in my spirit as the words vibrate deep down in my soul. I still hear the words — victory, victory, sweet, sweet, victory!

"Take back your authority, war in the name of Jesus, by applying the blood of Jesus over your life and the life of your loved ones. Break the power of the enemy, be free from limitations, addictions, depression, sickness, and diseases. Replace sadness and distress with the joy of the Lord."

Round Eight

The Truth

The truth will set you free.

"Then you will know the truth, and the truth will set you free."
John 8:32

A dream? This was all a dream? It felt so real and I feel like a new man. I had the wrong impression of God. I thought He caused all my problems, especially the death of my wife and all of my financial issues. It is God who causes me to triumph. It is He who causes me to gain wealth. The accident was not my fault.

Now that I know the truth, I realize this fight represents the warfare. The ring is where I have been boxed in nursing my dilemmas and struggles. The beast is the invisible foe we fight. He embodies all fears and what is negative in my life.

The trainer is the person or persons in my life that will lead me to the truth of God. The referee is the indivisible power: The Holy Spirit. He is also the inside voice who taught me to war and control the forces of the enemy in my life before I even knew there was a greater power.

Now I am coupled with the greater power–*the Lord Jesus Christ*. I want to take back all the years I have allowed fear and depression to constrain my actions. The only way to overcome my fears is to take action. I will fight fear, doubt, and unbelief with the bible that declares the Word of God of who I am in Christ and take my rightful position in life. I am seated with Christ Jesus in heavenly places. I am determined now more than ever to fight the low self-image that my negative words have produced. I am determined to fight for my dreams. I am determined to be consistent and persistent in my positive affirmation to live the life of a winner. I will no longer allow my feelings to fool me. I will change the way I see life by changing the atmosphere with positive words. I will face my fears head-on to conquer them. I will change my mindset by reading the Word of God – the Bible. I will become the person God has called and designed me to be. I will allow my body to be a living temple for the Lord, instead of a punching bag for negativity. I will always give Him the glory and praise.

I am a winner with Jesus Christ, and I have a winner's attitude.

INVITATION

You, too, can have a winner's attitude with Lord Jesus Christ on your side. Invite Jesus in your heart today by repeating:

Dear Heavenly Father, I come to you in the name of Jesus. Your Word says, "Him that cometh to me I will in no wise cast out." So, I know you will not cast me out, but you will take me in, and I thank you for it. You said in your Word, "If thou shalt confess with thy mouth the Lord Jesus and shall believe in thine heart that God hath raised Him from the dead, thou shalt be saved". For whosoever shall call upon the name of the Lord shall be saved." I believe in my heart that Jesus Christ is the Son of God. I believe He rose from the dead for my justification. I am calling upon His name–the name of Jesus. Father, I know I am saved now. Romans 10:10 states, "With the heart man believeth unto righteousness: and with the mouth, confession is made unto salvation"

I believe with my heart, and I confess Jesus now as my Lord Thank you, Father.

(John 6:37) (Romans 10:9,13)

Decision

You must make the decision.

If you repented of your sins and received Christ today, welcome to God's family! Your goal now is to grow closer to Him.

"For now, we live, if ye stand fast in the Lord."
(1 Thessalonians 3:8)

Jesus never promised this life would be easy, but He promised a way of escape and freedom.

"No temptation has overtaken you that is not common to man. God is faithful, and he will not let you be tempted beyond your ability, but with the temptation he will also provide the way of escape, that you may be able to endure it." (1 Corinthians 10:13)

"Now, you fight the good fight of faith." (1 Timothy 6:12)

Now, you fight the good fight of faith, for you have a God-given right to stay free.

> *"For, brethren, ye have been called unto liberty; only [use] not liberty for an occasion to the flesh, but by love serve one another,"* **(Galatians 5:13)**

> *"Let us hold fast the profession of our faith without wavering, for he is faithful that promised."* **(Hebrews 10:23)**

You must understand this fight is not a physical one, but spiritual.

> *"For we wrestle not against flesh and blood, but against principalities, against powers, against the rulers of the darkness of this world, against spiritual wickedness in high places."* **(Ephesians 6:12)**

Your fight is against an ancient invisible foe; Please do not take him lightly. **Ephesians 2:2** states:

> *"Wherein in time past ye walked according to the course of this world, according to the prince of the power of the air, the spirit that now worketh in the children of disobedience."*

Since you have changed your citizenship, you are seated with Jesus in heavenly places and you war from this realm. Jesus is seated at the right hand of the Father.

Ephesians 1:19–23:

And what is the exceeding greatness of his power to us-ward who believe, according to the working of his mighty power, which he wrought in Christ, when he raised him from the dead, and set him at his own right hand in the heavenly places, far above all principality, and power, and might, and dominion, and every name that is named, not only in this world, but also in that which is to come: and hath put all things under his feet, and gave him to be the head over all things to the church, which is his body, the fullness of him that filleth all in all.

He walked this earth with the power of the Holy Spirit and when He left, He gave unto us the same power to walk over the enemy. Do not be confused or dismayed. When things go haywire, keep your focus on Jesus. Like Paul, you must be persuaded:

"For I am persuaded, that neither death, nor life, nor angels, nor principalities, nor powers, nor things present, nor things to come, nor height, nor depth, nor any other creature, shall be to separate us from the love of God, which is in Christ Jesus our Lord."
(Romans 8:38-39)

Learn the voice of God over all other voices; to discern His voice. You must *spend valuable time in prayer and in His Word.* Prayer is important because it is communicating with your Heavenly Father for clear direction and gives Him permission to work on your behalf. Reading His Word tells you who you are in Christ. You will then learn how to pray and learn His laws and precepts, which will become your weapons of warfare against the enemy. To break the power of your enemies, you must stay in the presence of the Almighty God; this will help you continue to grow! They will know you by your fruit:

> *"But the fruit of the Spirit is love, joy, peace, longsuffering, gentleness, goodness, faith, meekness, temperance: against such there is no law."*
> **(Galatians 5:22-23)**

As soon as Christ comes into your life, you take on the fruit of the Spirit. I have found one of the greatest ways to destroy the spirit of depression is with the spirit of joy. Spiritual joy is a deep cheerfulness and gladness of heart. It is happiness and a calm spirit. It comes to us as the direct result of knowing Christ Jesus intimately, along with all He has done and will do for us. Christ has given us a permanent joy, saying:

> *"Your joy no man taketh from you."* **(John 16:22)**

Decision

Paul gives powerful orders to

> *"Rejoice in the Lord always."* (1 Thessalonians 5:16).

Verse 18 says:

> *"In everything give thanks; for this is God's will for you in Christ Jesus."*

Sometimes it may be hard to rejoice, but that does not change the command. It is God's will we find joy in prayer. Pray about every situation, and there should be no circumstances in your life where you cannot give thanks.

> *"God works everything together for the good of those who love Him."* **(Romans 8:28)**

You should rejoice, pray, and give thanks in all things. This is the will of God, for every believer in every situation, and it activates spiritual joy. The apostle Paul was in prison in Rome and still wrote:

> *"Rejoice in the Lord always; again I will say, rejoice!"* **(Philippians 4:4)**

Not once, but he repeats it. You must and should rejoice, for it is necessary for your deliverance to remain. Paul commanded you to be happy and rejoice in the Lord.

Rejoice in the Lord

You are to "rejoice in the Lord," not your circumstances. Your rejoicing is to take place in Christ. You are to take delight in Him. Your example is in the apostle Paul, for he had inner fortifying joy when his external circumstances looked bleak.

Whatever happens from this day forward, *"rejoice."* Rejoicing is something every Christian should do, regardless of the changes and circumstances that come into their lives. That is the attitude every believer in Christ should have. Everything that matters in this life, put it on the altar and give it to Christ. If you trust in Jesus Christ, the whole covenant of grace is yours. You have a right to everything that grace provides as a co-inheritor with Jesus Christ. The Psalmist said:

"Delight yourself also in the Lord." **(Psalm 37:4)**

Did you give your life to Jesus Christ?

Then Rejoice in Him!

Other Books From Change Publishers

Coming Soon From Change Publishers

For a complete list of our titles,
visit us at www.changepublishers.com.

Columbia, South Carolina

changepublishers@gmail.com

www.ingramcontent.com/pod-product-compliance
Lightning Source LLC
Chambersburg PA
CBHW071035080526
44587CB00015B/2623